WORLD OF KNOWLEDGE
PREHISTORIC TIMES

BELITHA PRESS

This edition published in 2003 by
Belitha Press
A member of Chrysalis Books plc
64 Brewery Road, London N7 9NT

Typeset by Chambers Wallace, London
Printed in China
British Library Cataloguing in Publication Data
for this book is available from the British Library.

ISBN 184138 601 4

Acknowledgements

Photographic credits:

Bridgeman Art Library 9 top, 11 top
ET Archive 10
Geoscience Features 15, 20, 28
Robert Harding Picture Library 18, 47
Michael Holford 8/9
NHPA 23 top, 31, 37 top, 48 bottom
Natural Science Photos 5, 11 bottom, 14, 17, 19, 23
    bottom, 24 left, 29, 34, 35 bottom, 37 bottom, 41,
    48 top, 51, 56, 57 right
Nigel Press 7
Oxford Scientific Films 8 left, 12 top and bottom
    right, 33, 42, 44
Ann Ronan Picture Library 12 left, 13
Planet Earth 24 right, 26, 30, 32, 35 top

Illustrated by: David Holmes and Eugene Fleury

This book is based on an original text by: Theodore
Rowland-Entwistle

Series editor: Neil Champion
Educational consultant: Carolyn Kain
Editorial: Dee Turner and Kate Scarborough
Designed by: Groom and Pickerill
Picture research and art editing: Ann Usborne
Specialist consultant: the late Dr Gwynne Vevers

Contents

Words found in **bold** are explained
in the glossary on pages 60 and 61

CHAPTER ONE
PLANTS AND ANIMALS

The Variety of Life

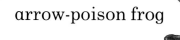

humming-bird

Our world teems with living things. There are about 350,000 different known kinds of plants and over one million kinds of animals. Some living things, such as **bacteria**, are neither plants nor animals. Each different kind of living thing is called a **species**. Scientists give each species a Latin name. Latin names are used because many plants and animals have the same common name. For example,

ground squirrel

starfish

angel-fish

arrow-poison frog

'robin' is the common name for at least eight species of birds.

Evolution

Evolution is the way in which new species develop. This process has been going on for millions of years. The earliest traces of living things ever found were the remains of some **algae**. These tiny life forms lived about 3,800 million years ago. Several species of animals have become **extinct** fairly recently. For example, the passenger pigeon died out in 1914. Many other species are in danger of extinction. These include the Bengal tiger and the giant panda.

fungus

beetle

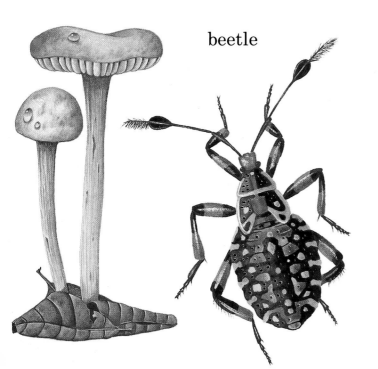

▲ The orang-utan is in danger of extinction. Only 5,000 are still alive.

Classification

Scientists put all living things into a series of groups. All animals are members of the animal kingdom. This is broken down into smaller and smaller groups. The tiger, for example, is described as follows:

Group	Latin	English
kingdom	*Animalia*	animals
phylum	*Chordata*	vertebrates
class	*Mammalia*	mammals
order	*Carnivora*	carnivores
family	*Felidae*	cats
genus	*Panthera*	big cats
species	*tigris*	tiger

For short, scientists refer to the tiger as *Panthera tigris*.

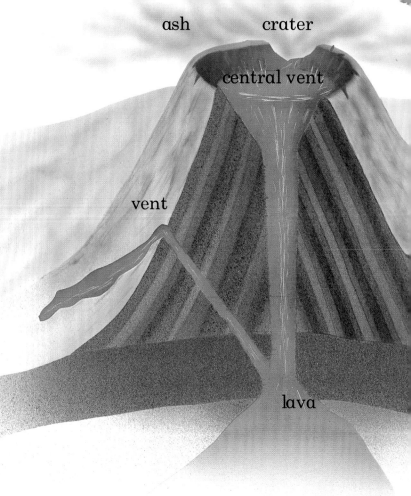

ash   crater

central vent

vent

lava

A Changing World

▶ A volcano builds a cone of ash and lava around its central vent, where a crater forms.

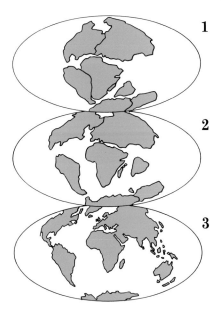

1

2

3

▲ The maps show the Earth (**1**) 180 million years ago, (**2**) 65 million years ago and (**3**) today.

The Earth is one of nine **planets** that go around the Sun. It is the only planet we know of that has life on it. The Earth is changing all the time. The rock deep inside the Earth is so hot that it is **molten**. Volcanoes form in places where some of this molten rock comes to the surface. And earthquakes shake some areas of the Earth. Both rain and wind wear away the land. We call this **erosion**. And rivers carry soil from the land to the oceans.

▲ A picture from a satellite showing the delta of the river Nile. The area where plants grow has been coloured red-brown.

The land divides

About 200 million years ago, all the land was together in one huge mass called Pangaea. This broke up into **continents**, which are still slowly moving apart. The continents move because they ride on huge, slowly drifting plates that make up the Earth's surface. When one plate rubs against another one, it can push up mountains or cause earthquakes. Earthquakes occur when plates that are jammed together suddenly break free.

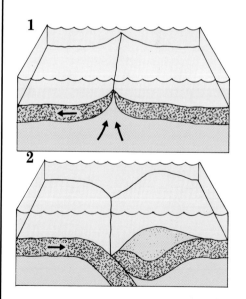

▲ Molten lava along a mid-ocean ridge pushes the sea floor plates apart (1). One plate edge sinks beneath the other (2).

7

Evolution or Creation?

Most scientists today believe that all living things have developed from simple life forms that lived millions of years ago. This is called evolution. However, some people think that living things were created in their present form by God, or perhaps by many gods.

Some creation stories

The Hebrew writers of the Book of Genesis said that God created Heaven and Earth out of a vast ocean. Some legends of the North American Indians tell of a crab, fish, or tortoise that made land out of mud from the sea. Pacific islanders thought the world slowly came out of emptiness.

▲ Evidence of ancient life is found in rocks. These dinosaur bones are millions of years old.

◄ A picture by the artist and poet William Blake (1757-1827). It shows God marking the circle of the Earth with a golden compass.

Ancient Vikings believed that the god Odin killed Ymir, a giant. Then Odin formed the land and sea from the body of the giant.

◄ The story of the Great Flood appears in many legends. This scene from Mesopotamia (now Iraq) dates from about 2,300 BC. It shows the animals being saved from drowning.

9

Darwin's Theory

▼ HMS *Beagle*, the ship in which Charles Darwin sailed in the 1830s. Darwin's theory helps explain how life evolved in prehistoric times.

In December 1831, a 22-year-old British **naturalist** named Charles Darwin joined a scientific expedition. He sailed around the world in a small ship, HMS *Beagle*. The journey took nearly five years. During the voyage, Darwin became very interested in a group of birds called finches. These lived on the Galapagos Islands, off the coast of South America. Darwin noticed that all these finches were very much alike. But their beaks seemed to be shaped to help different groups of birds to eat different foods.

◄ Charles Darwin was 50 years old when this picture of him was painted. At this time, he was completing his theory of evolution.

Natural selection

Darwin thought that all these birds must be **descendants** of just one kind of finch. He thought about this for 20 years. He knew that farmers could breed improved cattle by carefully selecting the parents. So it seemed likely that some natural process might have caused the changes in the finches. Darwin called this process natural selection. This is the basis of our ideas of evolution.

▼ Over the centuries, farmers have bred many kinds of cattle.

wild white

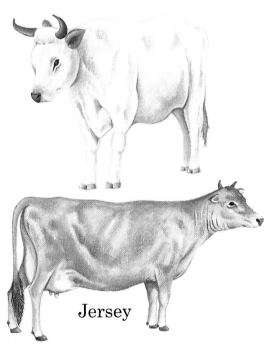

Jersey

◄ The medium ground finch, one of the Darwin's finches from the Galapagos Islands. It has a short beak for eating seeds.

Mendel's Method

In the 1800s, an Austrian monk called Gregor Mendel, did some important experiments with plants. He **bred** different kinds of pea plants together and noted what the new plants were like. These experiments showed how new plants get some features from the parent plants. This process is called **heredity**.

Many features of animals are

► The light peppered moth lives on light-coloured trees. The dark variety lives on dark trees. Birds soon catch any moths that settle on the wrong trees.

▲ Gregor Mendel experimented with plants in a monastery.

◀ The middle flower is a cross between the pink and white ones.

Survival

Animals do not change so that they can survive. But they may survive because they have changed. For example, the city-dwelling peppered moth survived because it had become dark, thus matching its dirty background. If it had remained light in colour, it would have been easy prey for birds in cities.

inherited too. In humans, these include the colour of the skin and eyes.

Genetics

Plants and animals are all made up of tiny cells. These contain parts called **genes**. It is the genes in the parents' cells that control the features that a plant or animal inherits. The study of genes is called genetics.

▼ The mountain king snake (left) is harmless. Its enemies keep away because it looks like the poisonous coral snake (right). This means of survival is called protective coloration.

Rocks

CHAPTER TWO

CLUES TO THE PAST

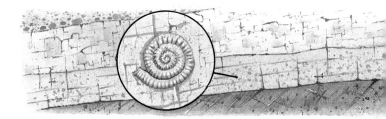

▶ In a wall of the Grand Canyon in Arizona, USA, is an example of rock strata that formed over many years.

There are three main kinds of rocks. Igneous rock comes up hot and molten from inside the Earth. Sedimentary rock is made from rock pieces that have stuck together and hardened to make fresh rock. And metamorphic rock is made when other rock changes because of heat, pressure and chemical action inside the Earth.

Glomar Challenger

This special drilling ship has been taking samples of sedimentary rock from ocean beds. The rock tells us about Earth's history.

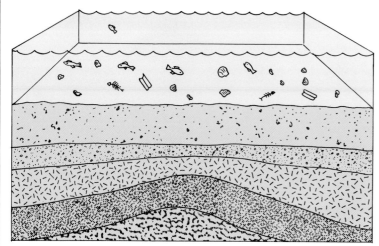

▲ These layers of rock formed at different times. Many layers contain fossils.

◄ Deposits of oil and natural gas can become trapped under layers of rock. Oil is formed from the bodies of tiny prehistoric sea animals.

Layers of rock

Sedimentary rocks form over millions of years in layers, or strata. Usually, the top layer is the newest and the bottom layer is the oldest. Many of these rocks contain the remains of animals and plants that lived when the rocks were forming. We can learn about the history of the Earth from them.

▲ Rock samples drilled out from great depths.

Fossils

We know about **prehistoric** life because the remains of many plants and animals have been preserved as **fossils**. Some fossils are only a few thousand years old. But others formed millions of years ago. Most fossils form in various kinds of sedimentary rock.

How fossils form

Fossils form in various ways. If a dead animal sinks in water, dissolved minerals may get into its bones or shell. These minerals

▼ Different kinds of fossils are found in rocks of different ages.

may later harden to form stone. This will **preserve** the bones or shell of the animal.

Sometimes water dissolves the body of a plant or animal. This leaves a hollow mould. Minerals may then fill the mould and harden to form a stone copy of the original.

Trace fossils are marks left by animals long ago. They include footprints left in mud that has since hardened.

▲ A fish fossil about 100 million years old.

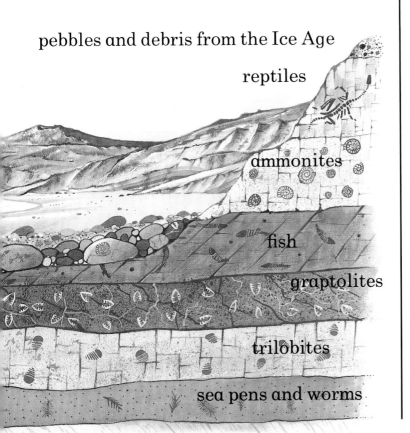

pebbles and debris from the Ice Age

reptiles

ammonites

fish

graptolites

trilobites

sea pens and worms

Living fossils

● The coelacanth is a fish thought to have died out 65 million years ago. Then one was caught off the coast of South Africa in 1938.

● The ginkgo is a tree that grows in China and Japan. It is the only survivor of a group of plants that grew 200 million years ago.

● Horsetails are plants that have changed little over 300 million years.

● The Virginia opossum is an animal that has hardly changed in the past 36 million years.

Finding Fossils

▶ Fossil logs 200 million years old lie in Petrified Forest National Park, Arizona, USA. Their wood has turned to stone.

Famous sites

● The Dinosaur National Monument in Colorado, USA, contains fossil remains of dinosaurs and other prehistoric animals.

● Olduvai Gorge in Tanzania, Africa, contains many fossil remains of early humans. Some of these fossils are about two million years old.

● Rancho La Brea, in Los Angeles, USA, is the site of pits where thousands of animals were trapped in pools of tar over two million years ago.

Most fossils are found in places where there are exposed **sedimentary** rocks. Scientists often search for fossils in the sea, by rivers, in the walls of quarries and in coal mines. Indeed, coal itself is a fossil. It was formed from ancient forests.

◄ Collecting fossils is a slow process requiring a great deal of patience. Here, a collector is brushing dirt from the fossil of an ichthyosaur – a sea reptile with a body like a porpoise.

Scientists studying fossils note the various kinds of remains that are found together. Human skeletons near a group of animal bones may show that our ancestors used to eat certain kinds of animals. A fossil group found together like this is called a life assemblage.

Beware!

If you hunt fossils, go with a parent or teacher. Near cliffs or quarries, wear a hard hat as protection from falling rock. Near the sea, watch for rising tides.

Dating rocks

Radioactivity helps scientists to learn the age of rocks. Many rocks contain radioactive elements that change very slowly into other elements. The time it takes to do this helps scientists work out the age of a rock.

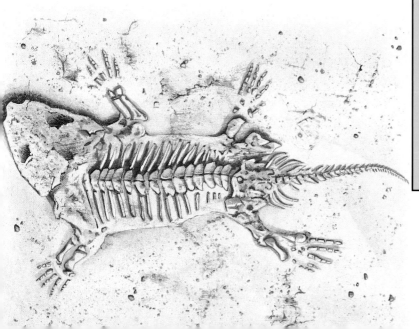

◄ The complete fossil skeleton of a long-dead animal.

Rebuilding Skeletons

It takes a lot of knowledge and skill to put a collection of scattered bones together to build up a skeleton. Much depends on how carefully the fossils are dug out. Scientists use photographs, drawings and notes to show how the bones were lying when found.

It may take months of work in a laboratory to rebuild a fossil skeleton. Workers first clean the bones and piece them together. If some bones are missing, the scientists may use plaster copies of other bones.

Sometimes, scientists make

The iguanodon

In 1878, a patch of sand full of huge bones was found in a Belgian coal mine. The complete skeletons of more than 30 iguanodons were dug out and re-assembled. An iguanodon thumb bone is the size of a rhinoceros horn.

► This painting shows what plants and animals may have looked like in the Cretaceous period, 65-140 million years ago.

lifelike models of ancient animals, such as the dinosaur. It is fairly easy to work out the shape of the body. For the scientists know where the muscles would have to go to make the animals move. But they can never be sure what kind of skin or fur the animals had.

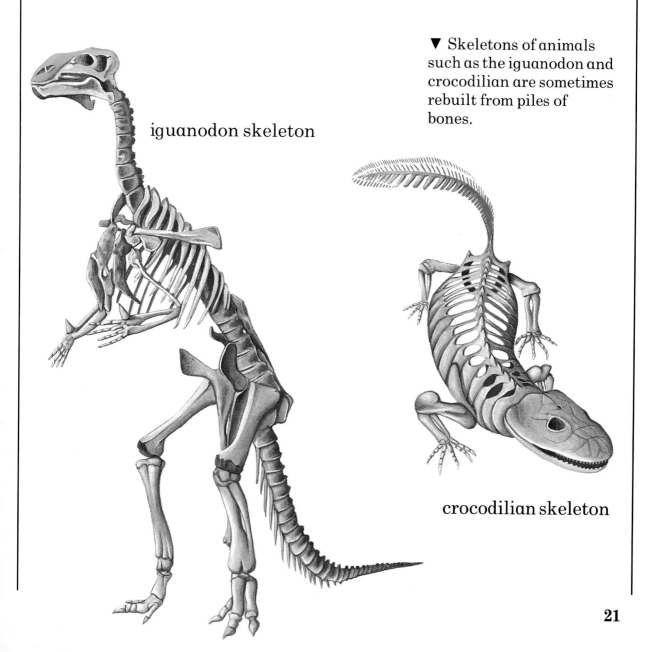

▼ Skeletons of animals such as the iguanodon and crocodilian are sometimes rebuilt from piles of bones.

iguanodon skeleton

crocodilian skeleton

Land and Sea

CHAPTER THREE

THE EARLY DAYS

The Earth is about 4,600 million years old. In its early days, the Earth was a hot place with many volcanoes that hurled out **lava**. They also pumped out great amounts of steam and other gases. As the Earth slowly cooled, the steam turned into water to form the oceans, just over 4,000 million years ago.

Mountains
Some mountains are built up by volcanic action. Larva flowing

▼ In its early days, Earth's many volcanoes spouted clouds of steam and gases. The steam condensed to form rain that slowly collected to form the oceans. There were often violent thunderstorms.

down the sides of a volcano cools and becomes solid. So the volcano gradually becomes bigger over the years.

Fold mountains are formed by slow, but powerful movements of land masses. The enormous pressure buckles the land to form mountains and valleys. The Himalayas and Alps were formed in this way.

Block mountains occur where forces in the Earth's surface push some blocks of land upwards. Steep-sided valleys form where blocks slip down.

▲ The Himalayas (top) were formed from folds in the land. This peak in Malawi (above) is a block mountain.

How Life Began

Life could not begin on land because there was not enough **oxygen** in the **atmosphere**. We now think that life began in the oceans. Simple chemicals reacted together to make more complex substances, including proteins.

These joined with other complex substances to make simple living cells. Some of these cells joined together to form more complex life forms. Over thousands of millions of years, a huge variety of plants and animals evolved.

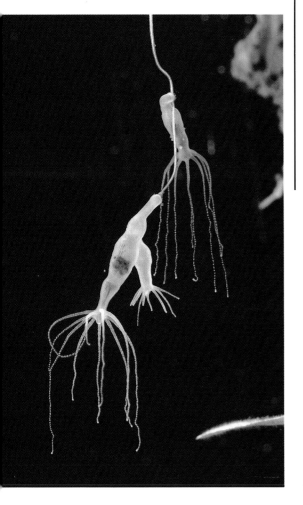

▲ The freshwater hydra began to evolve about 3,500 million years ago.

▶ A female deep-sea angler fish with two attached males.

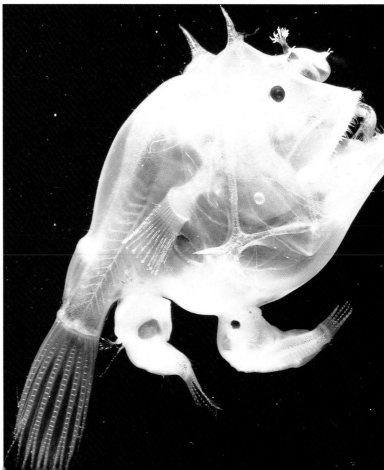

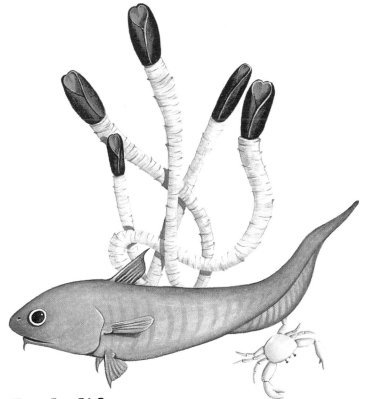

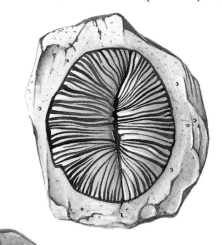

An old belief

People once believed that lifeless matter could turn into living things when soaked with rain and warmed by sunlight. This process was called spontaneous generation.

Early life

Some of the earliest traces of life come from South Africa and Canada. There geologists have found fossils, called stromatolites, that are about 3,500 million years old. Stromatolites are built up from layers of one-celled life forms called algae.

◄ Crabs and giant worms like this have been found deep in the ocean.

▼ These fossil sea animals were among the earliest known ocean dwellers.

Dickinsonia (worm)

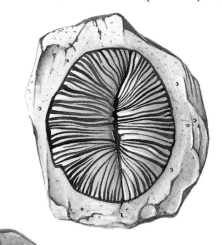

Charnia (sea pen)

Medusina (jellyfish)

Spriggina (worm)

25

Animals without Backbones

▼ Jellyfish are found in all the world's oceans.

Sea scorpion

The giant sea scorpion pterygotus was one of the most terrifying prehistoric creatures. It was over 2 metres long with a pair of claws and eight legs.

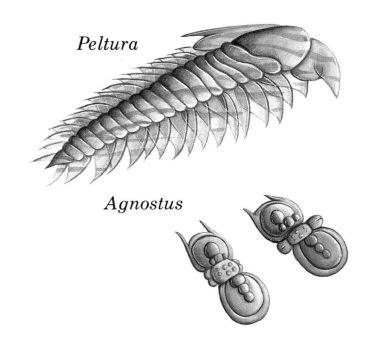

Peltura

Agnostus

Animals without backbones are called **invertebrates**. Even today there are many times more invertebrates than **vertebrates** – animals with backbones. As early invertebrates had completely soft bodies, few of their remains have been preserved as fossils in the rocks.

About 570 million years ago, animals began to develop hard parts, such as shells and chalky tubes. These are often found as fossils. One of the most common sea animals from this period was the trilobite. This small creature had a hard shell. Trilobites

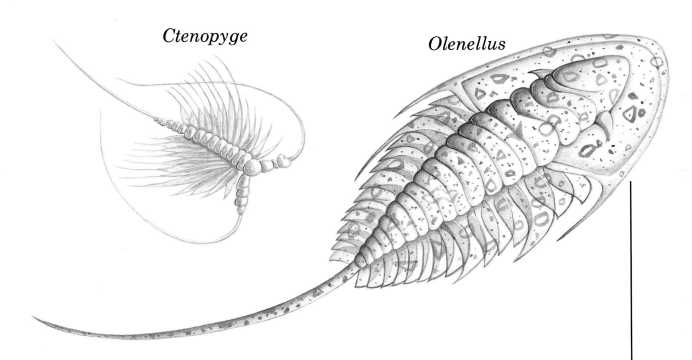

Ctenopyge

Olenellus

▲ Some prehistoric invertebrates.

belong to a group of animals called the arthropods. This group includes today's spiders, insects, crabs and lobsters. More than three-quarters of all animal species are arthropods.

Molluscs

There were also many molluscs in the sea. Many looked like molluscs found today. These include snails, oysters, scallops and octopuses. The ammonites are a group of molluscs that has died out. They had coiled shells. These varied in size from about five centimetres to nearly two metres across.

Groups of invertebrates

The main groups of invertebrates are listed below.

- Sponges
- Jellyfish and corals
- Comb jellies and sea gooseberries
- Molluscs, such as oysters, octopuses, slugs and snails
- Earthworms, leeches and lugworms
- Arthropods, such as lobsters, insects, spiders and crabs
- Starfish, sea urchins, brittle stars and sea cucumbers

Animals with Backbones

Animals that have backbones are called vertebrates. The backbone and the rest of the skeleton grow inside the animal's body. Vertebrates can grow much bigger than invertebrates because their bones can support a heavy weight. The skeleton keeps growing along with the animal. Most vertebrate skeletons have hard bones, but two groups of fishes have softer, tough **cartilage** instead. These fishes include lampreys and sharks. Some vertebrates, including turtles, armadillos and some dinosaurs, developed hard bony plates or shells.

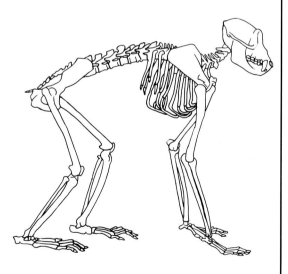

▲ A typical vertebrate skeleton, of a gorilla.

▶ A scene from 170 million years ago.

▲ A bull shark.

Brain power

A vertebrate's main nerves run inside its backbone, or spine. At the head end, these nerves enlarge to form a brain. A hard skull protects the brain from damage. The vertebrate's brain helps it do more complicated things than invertebrates, which do not have brains. Vertebrates also have skin that covers the entire body. The earliest fossils of vertebrates are about 500 million years old.

Groups of vertebrates

There are seven classes of vertebrates:

- Lampreys and hagfishes: fishes without jaws.
- Sharks and rays: fishes with cartilage, not bone
- Bony fishes
- Frogs, toads, newts and salamanders
- Reptiles, such as crocodiles, lizards, snakes, turtles
- Birds
- Mammals: animals that feed their young on milk; includes mice, whales and elephants.

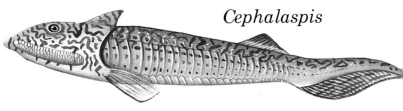

Cephalaspis

Bothryolepis

Fishes

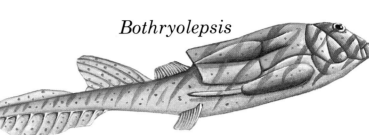

Tricky fossils

One group of fossil fish was found with their bodies curved instead of flat. At first, people thought the fish had been poisoned. Later, scientists realised that the fish had curled up when they dried out.

▼ A blue spotted ray, a fish with cartilage.

The first fishes swam in the seas about 500 million years ago. These fishes were the first vertebrates. Their skeletons were made of soft cartilage, not bone, so they formed very few fossils. Fishes with cartilage skeletons belong to the same group as today's sharks and rays. These early fishes had no jaws. Fishes with jaws appeared just over 400 million years ago.

Jamoytius

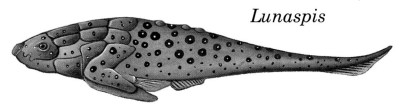

Lunaspis

◀ Fishes of the Silurian and Devonian periods. *Cephalaspis* and *Jamoytius* had no jaws. *Lunaspis* and *Bothryolepis* were early fish with jaws.

▼ Anatomy of a fish.

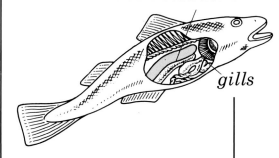

swim bladder

gills

Age of Fishes

By about 370 million years ago, fishes had become the most important animals in the sea. So this period, known to scientists as the Devonian period, is known as the Age of Fishes. By this time, bony fishes were common too.

There are many more bony fishes than there are other kinds of vertebrates, either in the sea or on land.

▼ A surgeon fish. It has a bony skeleton and lives among coral reefs.

31

CHAPTER FOUR
LIFE COMES ASHORE

The First Life on Land

▶ (opposite page) Frogs developed about 200 million years ago. This red-eyed leaf frog is from Costa Rica.
▼ A West African lung-fish.

About 400 million years ago, some plants and water animals moved from the seas to the rivers. At this time, sea plants were simple, one-celled organisms. The first large plants grew in swampy areas and peat bogs. In the next 100 million years, plants spread from the swamps and bogs until they covered much of the land.

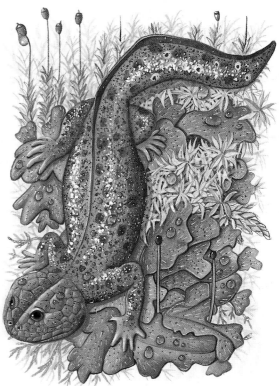

▲ Amphibians called labyrinthodonts died out about 190 million years ago.

Land animals

The first land animals were probably creatures with **jointed** legs – like today's insects and spiders. The first vertebrates to make their way on to land were the lung-fish. Such fishes still live in rivers and lakes. Lung-fish use gills to breathe in water, just like other fishes. But they also have lungs to breathe air. Their fins are fleshy stumps, which they use to 'walk' over the mud.

The next group to attempt life on land were the **amphibians**. Frogs are amphibians. They breathe air and live on land, but lay their eggs in water.

Groups of amphibians

There are three groups of amphibians living today:

● **Frogs and toads:** their strong back legs are good for jumping. The adults have no tails.

● **Salamanders and newts:** they have both legs and tails, but do not jump.

● **Caecilians:** these slim, legless, worm-like creatures live in the tropics.

Changing

▲ Moss and lichen can grow on a bare wall.

▼ A polar bear roams the Arctic. Its thick layer of fat and heavy fur help it survive the bitter cold.

As animals came to live on the land, they changed, or evolved, to fit into certain ways of living. For example, some birds slept in trees to avoid danger. Their legs evolved so that, when the birds relaxed, their claws would grip the branches tightly. This prevented them from falling while asleep. Other creatures, such as worms, developed a body for burrowing under the ground.

A place in the world

Every plant and animal has its place in the world. **Ecologists** are scientists who study plants and animals in the places where they live. Such places are called **niches**. Some niches are very

◀ Koalas live in eucalyptus trees in Australia. These feed on the leaves.

▼ Two lions, a male and a female, charge through African grassland. Groups of lions often hunt big animals.

general. For example, a rabbit will do well almost anywhere if there is a good supply of grass and other greens to eat. But some other life forms are much more specialized. A koala lives and feeds only on certain eucalyptus trees. Cacti thrive only in deserts. And mangrove trees grow only in swamps.

A tool for a bird

The woodpecker finch is one of the few birds that uses a tool to get its food. This bird has a short, stout beak, which it uses to chop into the bark of trees. It then uses a twig or a cactus thorn to scrape out insect grubs.

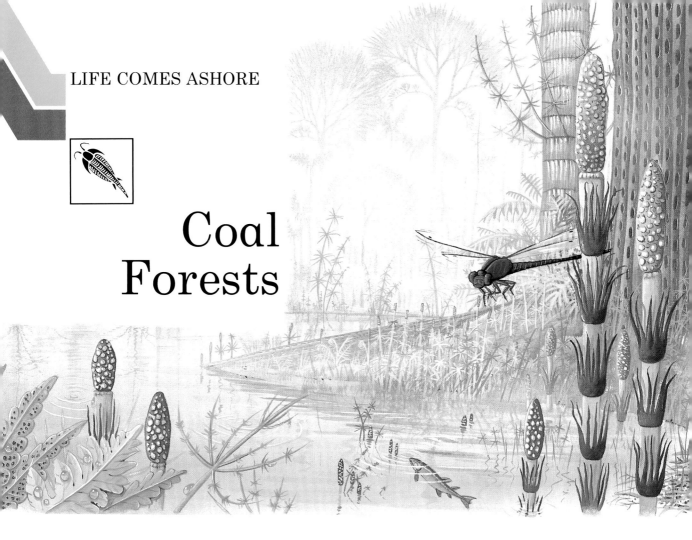

Coal Forests

▲ An artist's idea of a tropical swamp forest, 350 million years ago.

Kinds of coal

There are several types of coal. The most common is soft, bituminous coal. Hard coal, called anthracite, formed deep down under a lot of pressure. Lignite, or brown coal, formed more recently, closer to the surface.

Around 350 million years ago, huge **tropical** forests grew in swamps on land that later formed Europe, Asia and North America. Many of the trees were different from those that grow today. Some trees were club mosses that grew over 30 metres high. Today the club mosses are tiny plants. Other early trees were horsetails and giant ferns. The remains of these huge forests turned into the coal that is mined in many areas today.

How coal forms

When trees and other plants die in damp places, such as swamps, they rot and form a thick layer of decaying vegetable matter. In time, other material covers this layer. The buried material is pressed together, becomes hot and gradually forms peat. If this process continues, the peat slowly turns into coal. North America and the Soviet Union have huge areas of peat and coal. Among coal we often find the fossil remains of parts of plants. We may also find the remains of insects and other animals.

▲ Tree ferns such as this still grow in tropical lands.

▼ Peat is often very damp. These people digging peat will later dry it and use it for fuel.

Seeds

Some kinds of trees that grow today were already in existence 300 million years ago. They were **conifers**, such as pine, spruce and larch trees. These all bear seeds in cones. When ripe, the seeds blow away in the wind, assisted by their little 'wings'.

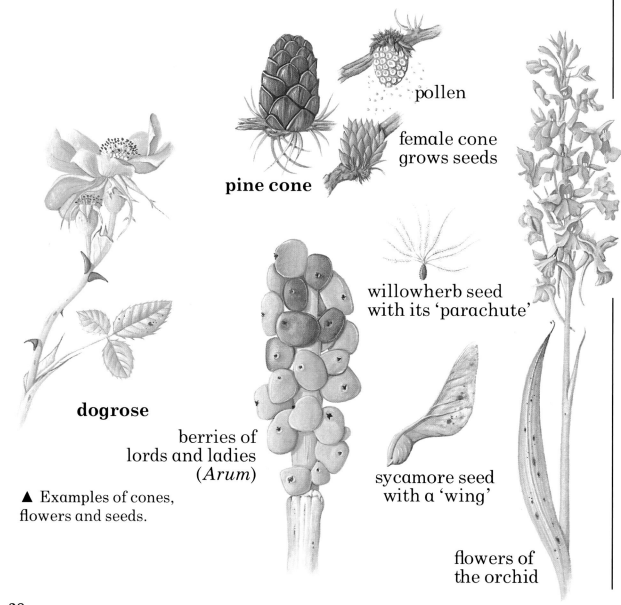

male cone produces pollen

pollen

pine cone

female cone grows seeds

willowherb seed with its 'parachute'

dogrose

berries of lords and ladies (*Arum*)

sycamore seed with a 'wing'

▲ Examples of cones, flowers and seeds.

flowers of the orchid

Flowers appear

Conifers were the main trees in the world's forests for about 200 million years. Then, just over 100 million years ago, flowering plants appeared. These plants protect their seeds inside their fruit. Flowering plants quickly spread all over the Earth. Now there are about 350,000 species of plants. Most food plants, including grasses, bear flowers.

Plants as food

These new plants brought a major change of food for the animals of that time. Although **mammals** had existed for about 100 million years, they became Earth's dominant animals only after the arrival of flowering plants. Many of these mammals evolved about 60 million years ago.

▲ A chestnut (left) splits open to free the ripe seed (nut) inside. A daffodil (above) has seeds growing inside.

▲ Insects are attracted to plants. But this plant, a sundew, eats insects.

Rulers of the Earth

CHAPTER FIVE

REPTILES

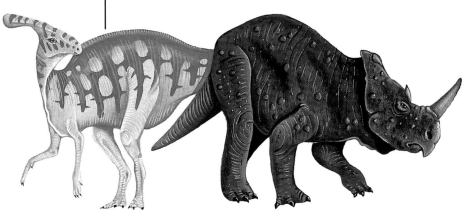

▲ Two dinosaurs, one duck-billed, one horned.

▼ A dinosaur, partly rebuilt to show how it fed.

The first true land vertebrates were **reptiles**. The eggs of a reptile have a protective skin, which stops them drying out. So they can be laid on the land. Many reptile eggs have a hard shell too. Reptiles probably evolved from amphibians, which lay their eggs in water. The first reptiles appeared about 300 million years ago.

The earliest reptiles looked a bit like crocodiles. Large and small **mammal**-like reptiles dominated the Earth about 250 million years ago. These died out about 230 million years ago. They left behind their descendants, the first true mammals. But reptiles still **dominated** the land.

Lizards

There were two groups of reptiles at this time. One reptile group was made up of early lizards. Most of these ate insects. The snakes evolved from this group of lizards. The other reptile group was made up of archosaurs. The archosaurs lived near water and ate fish. Some archosaurs evolved into dinosaurs.

▼ Snakes were the last group of reptiles to evolve. This Californian mountain kingsnake is warming up in the sun before it goes hunting.

◄ When it's hot, reptiles like this Nile crocodile rest in the shade to keep cool.

▼ Crocodiles have changed very little during the last 200 million years.

41

Dinosaurs

Bird-hipped dinosaurs

The dinosaurs with bird-like hips had very strange shapes. Some, like *Stegosaurus*, had plates and spines that protected them from meat-eaters.

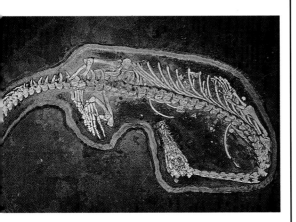

▲ This is a fossil skeleton of a *Mesosaurus*, a small, amphibious dinosaur.

▶ (opposite page) Some of the many kinds of dinosaurs.

The first dinosaurs appeared over 200 million years ago. The climate was warm and **humid**. Dinosaurs lived all over the land for 140 million years. The smallest was the size of a chicken, and the largest measured about 35 metres from head to tail.

Hip bones

There were two basic kinds of dinosaurs. One group had hip bones like modern lizards have. Some of this group, such as *Diplodocus* and *Brachiosaurus*, were huge, slow-moving plant-eaters that walked on four legs. Others, such as *Tyrannosaurus rex*, were meat-eaters that walked on large hind legs.

The second group of dinosaurs had hip bones like those of birds. Some dinosaurs in this group walked on their hind legs too. They had strong, beaked mouths with grinding teeth for eating plants. One group of bird-hipped dinosaurs, called hadrosaurs, had a bill like that of a duck, but with 2,000 teeth in it.

Rhamphorhynchus

Apatosaurus

Tyrannosaurus rex

Lesothosaurus

Compsognathus

Deinonychus

Prolercerta

David Holmes.

Swimming and Flying

▶ An ichthyosaur leaps and dives after fish. A plesiosaur swims under water. A flock of pteranodons looks for fish.

▲ Turtles have been around for 200 million years. The earliest were much like this Atlantic loggerhead turtle.

ichthyosaur

Some prehistoric reptiles swam in the oceans. There were two types of ocean-swimming reptiles: the ichthyosaurs, or 'fish-lizards', and the plesiosaurs, or 'near-lizards'. Both types of reptiles ate fishes.

In the air
About 230 million years ago, some reptiles began to glide through the air. They are called pterosaurs, meaning 'winged lizards', or pterodactyls, which means 'winged fingers'. They did not have true wings. But they

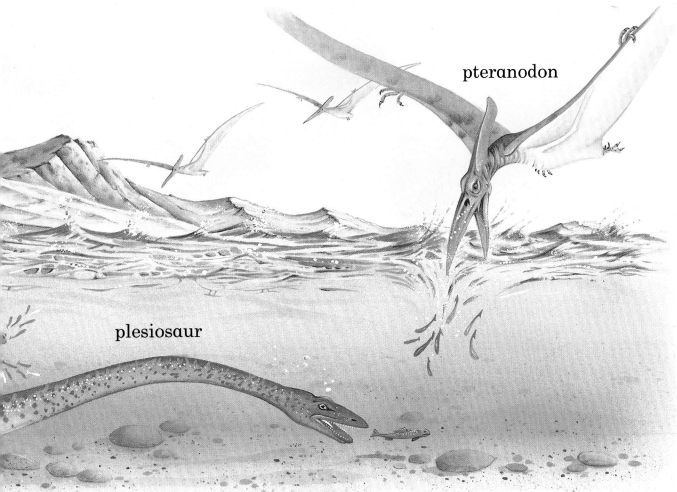

pteranodon

plesiosaur

had a fold of skin that stretched from the elbow to the knee on each side of the body. These first air reptiles lived in trees and glided to other trees or to the ground. Later pterosaurs had wings like those of modern bats. Early pterosaurs had teeth and long tails. But the later ones did not. One fossil pterosaur was found in the Soviet Union, complete with hairy skin. *Quetzelcoatlus*, the largest pterosaur, had wings that measured 10 metres, tip to tip.

Did you know?

Ichthyosaurs had bodies like those of dolphins and swam by paddling their flippers. They had long jaws with lots of teeth. They may have given birth to living young in the water. Plesiosaurs had bodies shaped like barrels. They swam through the water with a flying motion, like penguins. One group had long necks and small heads, with teeth to eat fish. Some plesiosaurs may have moved on land as well as in water.

Extinction

Dinosaurs die out

At least six mass extinctions have occurred in the past 500 million years. Two took place in the Permian and the Cretaceous periods. The first extinction lasted over many millions of years. Nine out of every ten sea creatures died out. The Cretaceous extinction killed the dinosaurs. It may have lasted only a few thousand years. The most recent mass extinction of species took place only two million years ago.

▶ More than one million animals live today. But many others lived in the past. They became extinct because they could no longer survive in their changing surroundings.

After ruling Earth for 140 million years, the dinosaurs suddenly died out. We know this because no dinosaur fossils were formed later than about 65 million years ago. Many other reptiles died out at the same time. Among them were pterosaurs, ichthyosaurs and plesiosaurs. But many other kinds of animals survived. These

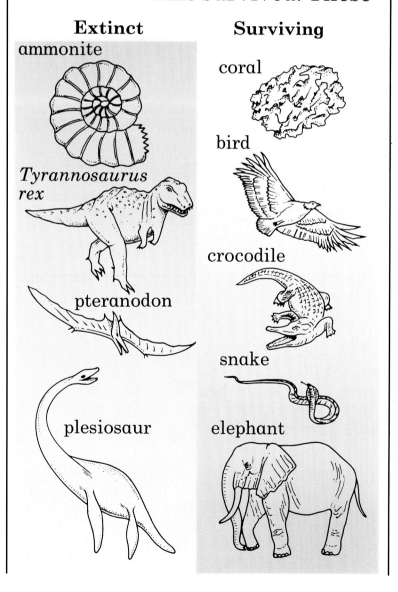

Extinct

ammonite

Tyrannosaurus rex

pteranodon

plesiosaur

Surviving

coral

bird

crocodile

snake

elephant

◄ Huge clouds of ash rose from Mount St. Helens volcano in 1980. Much bigger clouds came from Mount Tambora, when it erupted in 1816. Its dust stayed in the sky for about a year.

Killed by plants?

The spread of flowering plants over the world may have killed off the dinosaurs. Perhaps they could not eat these new kinds of flowering plants.

included mammals, crocodiles, snakes, amphibians and birds.

Possible causes

Many scientists believe that a change of climate killed off the dinosaurs. Huge **meteorites** may have struck the Earth, causing vast dust clouds. These could have blocked out the Sun's rays for years. Fossil remains show that dinosaurs lived on for a while in the tropics, after vanishing from the cooler parts of the Earth. As the dinosaurs died out, birds and mammals evolved more rapidly.

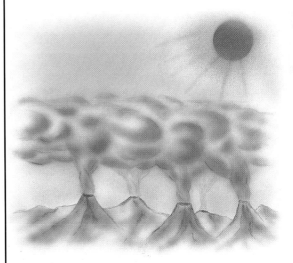

▲ Clouds of dust from volcanoes may have blocked out the sunlight, making it too cold for some animals and causing a mass extinction.

CHAPTER SIX

BIRDS AND MAMMALS

Birds

▲ An artist's idea of *Archaeopteryx*.

Birds evolved from reptiles. This is why some birds' legs have scales, like those found on reptiles. The first bird that we know of is called *Archaeopteryx*, which means 'ancient wing'. This bird was about the size of a pigeon, and it had feathers like a modern bird. But its bones were heavy, like those of a reptile. So *Archaeopteryx* may have been too heavy to fly.

Many of the early birds had teeth. One of them was *Hesperornis,* the dawn bird. This was a water bird that dived for fish. Dawn birds grew to two metres long and had 94 teeth.

Fish bird

Ichthyornis, the fish bird, was only about 20 centimetres long. It probably looked like a modern seagull.

▶ *Archaeopteryx* could probably jump off into the air, like this starling.

Flight

Less than ten million years later, birds had light, hollow bones and strong muscles. Now they could fly. It seems likely that *Archaeopteryx* could only glide down from the trees. But the lighter birds could take off into the air from the ground.

Flightless bird

Fossils of several giant birds have been found. *Diatryma* grew up to 2 metres tall. But it could not fly. It had a beak like a parrot and lived in what is now North America.

▼ Some of the birds that have died out.

Diatryma

Ichthyornis

Hesperornis

Archaeopteryx

Mammals

▲ This is an artist's idea of an early mammal. We don't know what many of them really looked like.

Did you know?

There are over 4,000 species of mammals. Some eat meat, some eat plants, some eat both.

A mammal is an animal that gives birth to live young and feeds them milk. The first mammals appeared about 230 million years ago and were very small. After the dinosaurs died out, bigger mammals evolved. Many were **marsupials**, like kangaroos. Such animals have pouches to hold their young.

Mammals take over

About 65 million years ago, mammals began spreading over the Earth. Mammoths and great cave bears appeared and later died out. Horses evolved first in North America. They died out there after they had spread to other parts of the world. Many mammals became sea animals. These include whales, dolphins, seals and porpoises. The first whales lived about 50 million years ago. Seals first appeared about 20 million years ago.

Groups of mammals

There are 18 orders of mammals:

- Egg-laying mammals, such as the platypus
- Marsupials, such as kangaroos and opossums
- Insect eaters, such as hedgehogs and moles
- Flying lemurs that glide, rather than fly
- Bats, the only mammals that truly fly
- Primates, such as apes, monkeys and humans
- Sloths and anteaters
- Pangolins
- Hares and rabbits
- Rodents, such as mice, beavers and squirrels
- Dolphins, whales and porpoises
- Carnivores, or meat-eaters, such as cats, dogs, wolves and bears
- Aardvarks
- Elephants
- Hyraxes
- Sea cows
- Odd-toed hoofed animals, such as horses
- Even-toed hoofed animals, such as cattle, pigs and camels

◀ The woolly mammoth died out 10,000 years ago. Complete frozen bodies have been found.

The Land Divides

About 180 million years ago, the land mass called Pangaea began to break up. The pieces slowly moved away from one another. These masses of land formed today's continents. The movement, which still continues, is called continental drift.

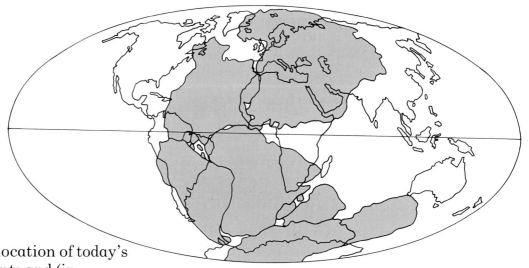

▲ The location of today's continents and (in orange) how they once formed.

Drifting dinosaurs

Dinosaurs drifted along with the continents. In the Jurassic period, *Stegosaurus* lived on in India, which was then an island, until it drifted into Asia.

Animals in isolation

When the continents drifted apart, changes in **climate** caused some plants and animals to die out. And many groups that survived were cut off from one another. When Australia became separated, only marsupial mammals lived there. These

duck-billed platypus

Tasmanian wolf

kangaroo

marsupials evolved to fill the niches that other mammals would fill elsewhere.

South America was once an island. Its animals included opossums and giant ground sloths. South America joined North America only about two million years ago. Then some animals from each continent moved to the other one. Opossums spread to North America and still live there.

▲ Because Australia is so far from other continents, many animals that have evolved there have not spread to other places. The three animals shown above are found only in Australia or nearby islands.

Humans Arrive

▼ The figures from left to right show how hominids evolved, from *Australopithecus* (the 'southern ape') to *Homo sapiens* – the 'wise man' of today.

Humans belong to a **family** of animals called the **hominids**. The oldest hominid fossil found so far was discovered in Africa. It is a $5\frac{1}{2}$ million-year-old *Australopithecus*, or southern ape (it is not a true ape).

Humans

Within the hominid family is a **genus** called *Homo*, or man. The earliest human species was *Homo habilis*, or handy man. It lived nearly 2 million years ago. Next

Australopithecus (southern ape)

Homo habilis (handy man)

▶ Comparing the skull of wise man with the skulls of other hominids. The word 'man' is used here to mean a species. It includes both males and females.

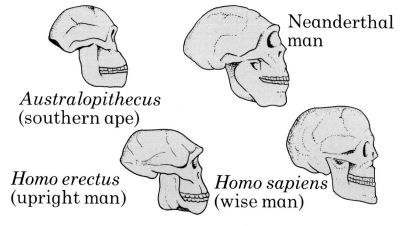

Australopithecus (southern ape)

Neanderthal man

Homo erectus (upright man)

Homo sapiens (wise man)

came *Homo erectus*, or upright man, which lived about 500,000 years ago.

All humans alive today belong to the species called *Homo sapiens*, or wise man. It first appeared about 300,000 years ago. A rugged form of wise man, called Neanderthal man, lived in Europe from about 75,000 to 35,000 years ago.

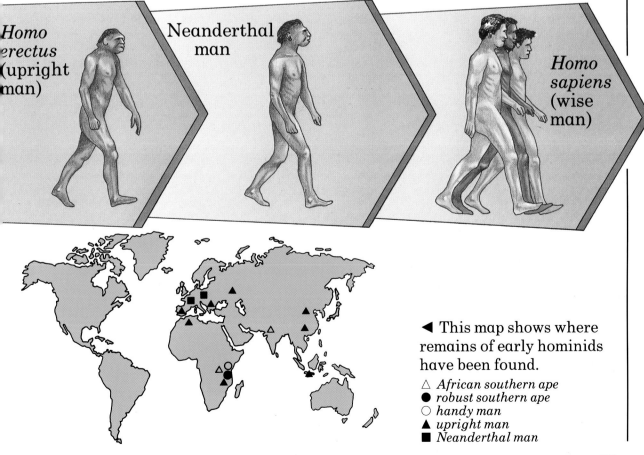

Homo erectus (upright man)

Neanderthal man

Homo sapiens (wise man)

◄ This map shows where remains of early hominids have been found.

△ *African southern ape*
● *robust southern ape*
○ *handy man*
▲ *upright man*
■ *Neanderthal man*

The Future

The study of prehistoric life shows us three things. First, humans evolved only recently in the history of the Earth. Second, the changes of evolution take place slowly. Third, evolution is still going on.

Humans rule the Earth, making changes everywhere. There is a danger that some changes that we make could lead to mass **extinctions**. We have already cut down half of Earth's tropical forests. If we destroy the homes of animals that live in the forest, they may die out.

▼ The Galapagos Islands in the Pacific are home to some species that are not found elsewhere.

Did you know?

More species of plants and animals are alive today than ever before. New species are still evolving.

◀ Many plants are rare, like this Chinese slipper orchid. People now try to protect rare plants and the places where they grow.

▼ Forest being cleared in Indonesia, with the loss of plants and animals.

Shaping the future

Scientists can now alter the cells of living things to bring about great changes in plants and animals. Our own future may change when colonies of people start to live on Mars or in space.

New species usually develop more quickly when a group of animals is left alone in a small area. So another species of human could eventually develop in space.

Time Chart of Earth's History

ERAS	PERIODS		MILLIONS OF YEARS AGO
			4600
PRECAMBRIAN (Before the Cambrian)		The longest period, nearly seven times as long as all the rest put together. The earliest forms of life developed in this period.	
			590
PALAEOZOIC (Ancient Life)	CAMBRIAN	Fossils include many sea animals. The first primitive fishes appeared towards the end of this period.	
			505
	ORDOVICIAN	The animal life was still in the sea. It included the trilobites.	
			438
	SILURIAN	The animal life in the sea included the trilobites and the sea scorpions. The first land plants appeared.	
			408
	DEVONIAN	Fishes became the most important animals in the sea. The first land animals (the amphibians) appeared.	
			360
	CARBONIFEROUS	Forests of giant tree-like ferns and horsetails flourished and their remains formed coal. The first reptiles appeared.	
			286
	PERMIAN	Amphibians, reptiles, mammal-like reptiles and modern kinds of insects flourished. A mass extinction at the end of the period killed off many sea animals, including the trilobites.	
			248

The Earth's long history is divided into four main lengths of geological time, called eras. Each era is divided into periods, and the two most recent periods are divided into epochs.

ERAS	PERIODS	EPOCHS		MILLIONS OF YEARS AGO
				248
MESOZOIC (Middle Life)	TRIASSIC	Large reptiles flourished, including the early crocodiles and dinosaurs, and the first mammals appeared.		
				213
	JURASSIC	The dinosaurs became dominant, while the mammal-like reptiles died out. The earliest-known bird, *Archaeopteryx*, lived towards the end of this period.		
				144
	CRETACEOUS	Dinosaurs were still dominant, while pterosaurs (flying reptiles) and primitive birds flew through the air. At the end of the Cretaceous period there was another mass extinction that killed off the dinosaurs and the ammonites.		
				65
CENOZOIC (Recent Life)	TERTIARY	Palaeocene	Many more mammals evolved.	
				55
		Eocene	The early horse appeared.	
				38
		Oligocene	Early apes appeared.	
				25
		Miocene	Apes became common.	
				5
		Pliocene	Ape-like men evolved.	
				2
	QUATERNARY	Pleistocene	Humans evolved.	
				0.01
		Holocene	Development of civilizations.	
				0

Glossary

Algae: certain simple plants that live in water, such as seaweeds.

Amphibians: animals that can live on the land or in the water. They lay their eggs in the water.

Atmosphere: the area that fills the sky and surrounds the Earth is the atmosphere. It is made up of invisible gases like oxygen.

Bacteria: these are very, very small living things, that can only be seen under a microscope. Some bacteria can make you ill.

Breed: a way of reproducing young from parents. These offspring will not be the same as their parents but will have some features that are alike.

Cartilage: a word for a kind of bone that is bendy and light, but very strong. Some fishes have a skeleton made from cartilage.

Climate: the usual type of weather a country or region has. For example, the Sahara desert has a hot and dry climate.

Conifer: a tree that produces cones, like pine trees.

Continent: a large area of land made of many countries. There are seven on Earth. These are Europe, Asia, North America, South America, Australasia, Africa and the Antarctica.

Descendants: these are people or animals who come from one set of parents. For example, you and your parents are descendants of your grandmother and grandfather.

Dominate: a word used to describe someone who is in control or masters others. For instance, a leader in a pack of wolves dominates all the others in that pack.

Ecologist: a person who studies plants and animals and where they live.

Erosion: this word is used to describe the way land is worn away by the wind and water. For example, cliffs are worn down by both wind and the sea.

Extinct: when all animals of the same kind have died out, that kind is extinct. For example, the last passenger pigeon died in 1914.

Family: a word used in science to describe a group of animals or plants that have features in common. For example a lion and a cat are from the same family.

Fossils: these are traces of past life forms that have been preserved in ancient rocks.

Genes: this word describes tiny little traces in the body that contain messages about certain features that may be passed on from a parent to a child. If your mother has red hair, she will pass that gene to you, so that you might have red hair. Even if you don't have red hair, you will carry her gene and your children might have red hair.

Genus: a word used to describe animals that have certain features in common. A lion shares certain features with other big cats, like the tiger and leopard. They all roar, and sit with their feet in front of them. They are put together in the same group called a genus.

Heredity: parents pass on certain features to their offspring. This process is called heredity.

Hominid: a human-like animal. For

example, an orang-utan is a hominid.

Humid: a word that describes weather that is warm and damp.

Invertebrate: an animal without a backbone.

Jointed: a knee allows you to bend your leg. This makes your leg jointed. Your elbow allows you to bend your arm. This means that your arm is also jointed.

Lava: a word that describes extremely hot rock that has become liquid which has forced its way out of the Earth through a volcano.

Mammal: a warm-blooded animal that feeds its young on its own milk.

Marsupial: a mammal that carries its young in its pouch.

Meteorite: a block of stone, coming from outer space, that strikes the Earth.

Molten: this word describes either metal or rock that has become liquid because of very great heat. Lava is molten rock.

Naturalist: someone who studies nature.

Niches: a word used in the study of nature to describe particular places where animals and plants live.

Oxygen: a gas that is colourless and invisible. It has no taste or smell. It is important for all animal and plant life on Earth.

Planets: these are large, solid bodies that move around the Sun. Mars and Mercury are planets.

Prehistoric: this word describes those events that belong to a time before history was written down.

Preserve: a way of stopping things from rotting or decaying. The Egyptians preserved human bodies which we call mummies.

Reptiles: cold-blooded animals with scaly skin.

Sedimentary: when bits of rock sink to the bottom of the sea and form a new rock layer, this rock layer is called sedimentary rock.

Species: this word describes a particular type of animal or plant. Lions are a species.

Tropical: a word used to describe hot and wet areas of the Earth.

Vertebrate: an animal with a backbone.

Index

A number in bold shows that the entry is illustrated on that page. The same page often has writing about the entry too.